THIS BOOK BELONGS TO:

_____

Every year, in April, families across Cambodia come together to celebrate Chaul Chnam Thmey, the Cambodian New Year. It's a time for joy, family, and tradition. Let's join Srey and her family as they prepare for this special time of year.

Before the New Year begins, Srey and her family clean their house from top to bottom. They hang bright lights and beautiful flowers to welcome the new year with a fresh start.

At the market, they buy new clothes and lots of delicious ingredients for special meals. Everyone is excited and busy preparing.

Srey helps her mom prepare the family altar with offerings for their ancestors and the Buddha. They place fruits, flowers, and incense as a sign of respect and gratitude.

On the first day of New Year, called Maha Sangkran, Srey and her family dress in their new clothes and visit the temple. They light incense and make offerings to the Buddha and their ancestors.

Srey bows with her hands together, saying a quiet prayer for a happy and prosperous new year.

As part of the Cambodian New Year celebrations, Srey and her family participate in the tradition of offering rice to the monks. Srey, holding a spoon, carefully scoops rice into a monk's bowl. Her parents are beside her, also making offerings.

With a tray full of delicious dishes, Srey carefully presents the food to the monks. The monks, dressed in their saffron robes, accept the offerings with gratitude.

This act of giving is a significant part of the New Year celebrations. It symbolizes generosity and respect, bringing blessings to Srey and her family.

Before enjoying the special New Year meal, the monks and the community come together in prayer. Srey and her family, along with other community members, sit respectfully in front of the monks, joining them in this solemn moment.

After the prayers, the community comes together to enjoy a delicious meal. Families, including Srey and her family, sit together at tables filled with traditional Cambodian dishes. The atmosphere is festive and joyful, with people talking, laughing, and sharing food. This moment of togetherness and sharing embodies the spirit of Cambodian New Year, bringing happiness and a sense of community to everyone involved.

On the second day, called Virak Vanabat, it's time to give back. Srey's family donates food and clothes to people who need them. Helping others is an important part of the New Year.

During the Cambodian New Year celebrations, Srey and her family enjoy watching a vibrant parade filled with music and costumes. Musicians play instruments, filling the air with joyous melodies, while dancers in vibrant costumes perform gracefully.

Srey and her family enjoy a vibrant performance featuring traditional Cambodian instruments and singers on stage. The musicians play beautiful melodies, while the singers, dressed in traditional attire, fill the air with captivating songs.
Below the stage, the crowd dances in a circle, adding to the festive atmosphere.

Srey eagerly visits food vendors selling a variety of Cambodian dishes and snacks. The bustling market is filled with the aroma of delicious foods.
Srey excitedly looks at the different stalls, each offering something unique and tasty.

Srey and her friends play traditional games 'Teanh Prot,' a tug-of-war game that everyone loves. It's all about teamwork and having fun.

Later, Srey's relatives come over for a big family reunion. They share stories, laugh, and enjoy a delicious feast together.

On the third day, called Tngay Leang Saka, Srey and her friends build sand stupas at the temple. These little sand towers are decorated with flowers and flags, representing the mountains where gods live.

Srey gently pours water over a Buddha statue using a flower, while her parents join her in this meaningful act.

The monks hold out their hands to be blessed. The temple courtyard is filled with other families participating in the ritual. This tradition symbolizes purification and brings blessings for the new year, strengthening the family's spiritual connection and sense of community.

The monks bless everyone with holy water, wishing them good luck and happiness. Srey feels refreshed and joyful.

Srey and her friends joyfully splash water and cover each other in baby powder, laughing and having fun together. This lively and playful activity is a favorite among children.

In the evening, Srey watches beautiful Apsara dancers perform.

As the New Year celebrations come to an end, Srey takes time to reflect on the past year. She thinks about her favorite memories and what she hopes to achieve in the new year.

Made in the USA
Las Vegas, NV
18 October 2024

10059659R00029